Growing a Plant:
A Journal

Contents

Week 1 3

Week 2 5

Week 3 7

Week 8 9

Week 12 11

Week 13 13

Week 15 15

Index 16

Rigby

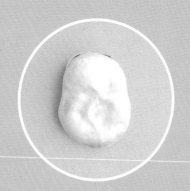

Week 1

I took one bean, some soil, and one glass.

I planted the bean.

I watered the soil.

Week 2

A root grew first.
Then a shoot grew.
Now it has a little leaf.

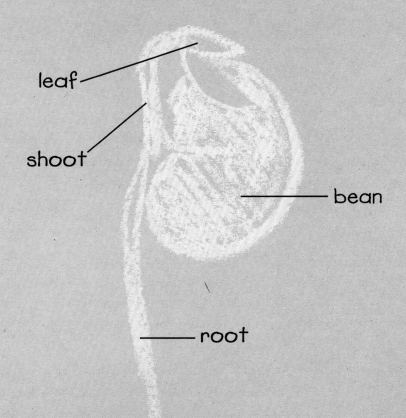

leaf

shoot

bean

root

Week 3

The shoot has come out
of the soil.
Now the leaves are opening.

——— leaf

shoot———

——— bean

roots ———

Week 8

The plant is 8 inches tall.
It is ready to plant
in the garden.

leaf

Week 12

Now the bean plant has a lot of flowers.

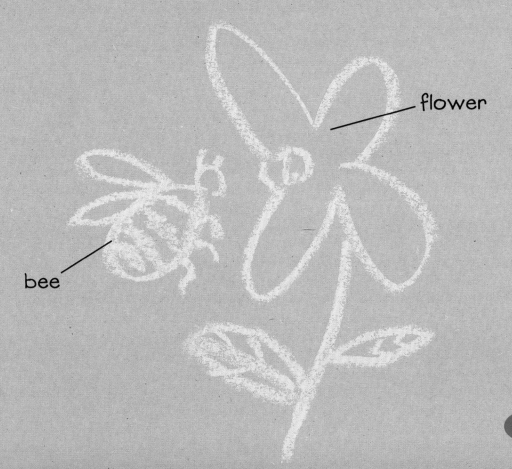

flower

bee

Week 13

The flowers have died.
Now there are little pods
where the flowers were.

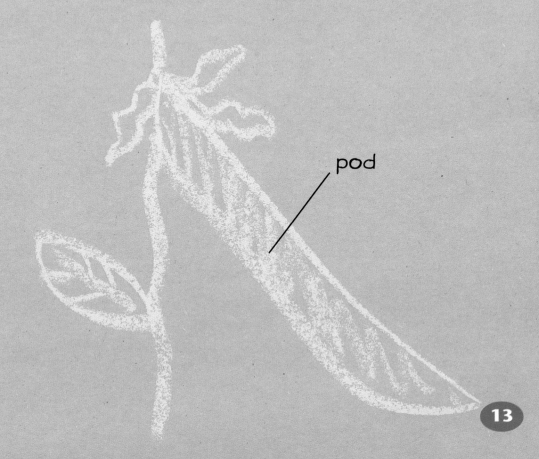

pod

Week 15

The pods have gotten bigger.
Inside there are some beans.
I can plant one of these beans
to make a new plant!

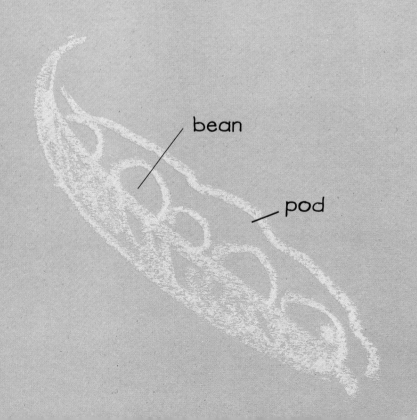

bean

pod

a
b
c
d
e
f
g
h
i
j
k
l
m
n
o
p
q
r
s
t
u
v
w
x
y
z

Index

 bean 3, 15

 bee 11

 flowers 11, 13

 leaf 5, 7, 9

 pod 13, 15

 root 5

 shoot 5, 7